Kevin sees a red balloon in the sky. It is drifting to the pond.

The balloon lands in the

pond. It floats on the water.

Kevin jumps into the water.

He sets off to get the balloon.

A goose sees the balloon too.

He sets off to get it.

Kevin gets to the balloon, but a puff of wind lifts it out of the water.

Kevin and the goose cannot reach the balloon. It floats away up into the sky.

The goose is cross. It hisses after Kevin all the way back to the grass.

Wellington is waiting for

Kevin on the grass. Yes!

He has got the red balloon.